Remembrance Day in Canada

written by
David James Pallister

illustrated by i Cenizal

Remembrance Day in Canada

Copyright © 2018 by David James Pallister

No part of this publication may be reproduced, distributed, or transmitted in any form or by any means, including photocopying, recording, or other electronic or mechanical methods, without the prior written permission of the author, except in the case of brief quotations embodied in critical reviews and certain other non-commercial uses permitted by copyright law.

The Poppy Design is a registered trademark of The Royal Canadian Legion, Dominion Command and is used under license.

Tellwell Talent
www.tellwell.ca

ISBN
978-1-77370-381-7 (Hardcover)
978-1-77370-380-0 (Paperback)

*To Peter, who always supports
my artistic projects.*

Remembrance Day is an important day for Canadians in early November. We chose this day to take time to remember all the men and women who have fought for Canada. It is important to remember all the people who worked so hard to keep Canada safe and free.

The **Poppy** is a part of Remembrance Day. It is a flower that grew on the battlefields and the graves of soldiers in World War One. We wear it to remember the men and women who died protecting Canada in wars.

The **wreath** is a part of Remembrance Day. It is a round decoration that we place on monuments during Remembrance Day ceremonies.

The **bugle** is a part of Remembrance Day. The bugle is a musical instrument similar to a trumpet. It is a long standing tradition from Great Britain to play The Last Post and Rouse during Remembrance Day ceremonies.

Soldiers are a part of Remembrance Day. They are the men and women in Canada's Armed Forces who have fought in wars to help keep us safe.

Veterans are a part of Remembrance Day. They are the men and women who fought in wars and lived to come back home with their sad memories of battles.

The Cenotaph is a part of Remembrance Day. It is a monument found in most Canadian towns and cities. The names of Canadian men and women who died in wars or battles are written on these monuments.

The **maple leaf** is a part of Remembrance Day. It is used to mark the graves of Canadian soldiers who died in Europe in World War One and World War Two.

The **National War Memorial** is a part of Remembrance Day. It is a special monument in Ottawa, Canada's capital city. People come from all over Canada to see it and to remember those who died to keep Canada safe.

The Memorial Chapel is a part of Remembrance Day. It is in a section of the Parliament buildings, called 'The Peace Tower', in Ottawa, Ontario. People visit there all year long to thank the men and women who gave their lives for Canada.

The Books of Remembrance are a part of Remembrance Day. They are located in the Memorial Chamber of the Peace Tower in Ottawa. In the books are the names of the Canadians who died keeping Canada safe in wars, so we can remain free.

The **number eleven** is a part of Remembrance Day. World War One ended on the 11th hour of the 11th day of the 11th month of 1918 and was called Armistice Day. This day and time (11:00am on November 11th) was chosen by the Canadian government for Remembrance Day. We take time every year to remember everyone who participated in wars to keep Canada safe.

NOVEMBER

SUN	MON	TUE	WED	THU	FRI	SAT
			1	2	3	4
5	6	7	8	9	10	11
12	13	14	15	16	17	18
19	20	21	22	23	24	25
26	27	28	29	30		

Speeches are a part of Remembrance Day. At Remembrance Day ceremonies, important politicians and other people share stories, talk about peace, and thank soldiers and veterans for their service to Canada.

The Two Minutes of Silence is a part of Remembrance Day. At 11:00 am on Remembrance Day, people stop to take special time to think of those who gave their lives for Canada.

CPSIA information can be obtained
at www.ICGtesting.com
Printed in the USA
LVHW072255151119
637560LV00011B/405/P